Umbre Everywhere!

Elora Grace

NEIGHBORHOOD
READERS

Rosen Classroom Books & Materials™

New York

"Jim, where is your umbrella?" said Mom.
"I lost it!" said Jim.
"Go find it," said Mom.

Jim went to look for his umbrella.
"Where is your umbrella?" said the girl.
"I lost it!" said Jim.
"I am looking for it."

"Where is your umbrella?" said the pig.
"I lost it!" said Jim.
"I am looking for it."

"Where is your umbrella?" said the dog.
"I lost it!" said Jim.
"I am looking for it."

"Where is your umbrella?" said the duck.
"I see my umbrella!" said Jim.
"It is in the water."

Jim went to his umbrella.
A fish was under the umbrella.
"Even a fish needs an umbrella today!"
said Jim.

Jim went home.
"Here is my umbrella!" he said.
"Where was it?" said Mom.
"A fish had the umbrella!" said Jim.